The Surname Cracknell

Dr Susan Morris &
Wendy Bosberry-Scott

ISBN: 1537013041
ISBN-13: 978-1537013046

The question of surnames, their origins, distribution and history, lies at the heart of genealogy as well as being fascinating in its own right.

In the 1980s and 1990s, long before many genealogical sources were even indexed, let alone online, our Surname Report service provided expert assessments of the origins, history and distribution of selected British surnames, using the sources available at the time.

Now, with so many more sources available, we believe that these reports retain their value as studies of individual surnames, and so we are gradually making the Debrett Surname Archive available online and in print for the first time. Some modern indexes have been consulted to refresh and update the reports.

Debrett Ancestry Research Ltd, PO Box 379,
Winchester SO23 9YQ
Tel: 01962 841904
Email: info@debrettancestry.co.uk
Website: www.debrettancestry.co.uk

CONTENTS

Overview

The use of surnames in England began in the Norman period, when surnames were not necessarily hereditary but usually a form of description. Some described the individual's trade or profession; others were nicknames; some gave the father's Christian name; others gave the individual's place of residence or origin.

Different surnames might be used in different documents, or more than one surname given in one document. Early descriptions were fairly elaborate and by the thirteenth and fourteenth centuries these were simpler, but still variable, and indeed the instability of surnames continued until well into the seventeenth century.

Although some Normans would already have had hereditary surnames on their arrival in Britain, the passing on of a surname from generation to generation only became customary in Britain gradually during the course of the thirteenth and fourteenth centuries. At the end of this period most of the population apparently had surnames.

Variations in the spelling of a family's surname continue to be found until the present century. Before this, as most people could not read or write, the parish clerk or other official would write down the name as they heard it.

There are four main groups of surnames:

A – Local names, which describe a person by his place of residence or origin.

B – Occupational names, which describe a person by his trade or profession.

C – Surnames of relationship, which refer to the Christian name of the father or other important relative.

D – Nicknames or sobriquets, coined to describe a person in terms of his appearance or character.

Many surnames have multiple origins, and the name Cracknell certainly falls into Category A, but as we will show, there has been a suggestion that it may also fall into Category B.

Origins and early examples

P H Reaney and R M Wilson's *Dictionary of English Surnames* (Oxford 1995), and Hank and Hodges' *Dictionary of Surnames* (Oxford 1992) agree that the surname Cracknell or Cracknall has a common root with the place-names Crakehall and Crakehill, which are both in north Yorkshire.

Eilert Ekwall's authoritative *Oxford Dictionary of English Place-Names* (4th edition, 1960) draws upon a national survey of early and secondary sources including charters, deeds, the Domesday Book and maps, to chart the various early forms of a given place-name and thus explain its meaning. His entry for Crakehall (Great and Little), Yorkshire, cites the Domesday Book (1086), where the place-name appears as *Crachele;* and A H Smith's work *The Place-names of the North Riding of Yorkshire* (Cambridge 1928), which notes a reference to *Crakehale* in 1157.

For the place-name Crakehill, Ekwall cites early examples from the Domesday Book (*Crecala*) and a Subsidy Return of 1301 (*Crakhale*).

Ekwall gives the meaning of both these place-names as '*hahl* [nook] frequented by the water crakes'. The more recent *Oxford Dictionary of English Place-names* (editor A D Mills, 2nd Edition, 1998), gives a similar explanation: 'Nook of land frequented by crows or ravens', from Old Scandinavian *Kraka* and Old English *Halh*.

3

However, A H Smith, the author of *The Place-names of the North Riding of Yorkshire* (1928), suggests an alternative derivation for the place-names Crakehall and Crakehill as 'Craca's nook', with 'Craca' being a personal name. Reaney and Wilson point out that the Old English for this would be *Cracanhale*, which is closer to the surname Cracknell but has not been found as a place-name in any record. The suggestion is therefore that the original form has survived in the surname but not the place-name. This is supported by the earliest example that has been found of the surname: Elias *de Crackenhal'* who appears in the Curia Regis Rolls of Yorkshire.

Earlier in the twentieth century, the surname scholar Ernest Weekley had presented a very different theory in *The Romance of Names* (1917):

> Craquelin, a cracknell; made of the yolks of egges, water, and flower; and fashioned like a hollow trendle (Cotgrave, *A Dictionarie of the French and English Tongues* (London 1611))

The *Oxford English Dictionary* defines cracknel as a 'light, crisp kind of biscuit, of a curved or hollowed shape', as described in a citation from 1503:

> Whan the plate is hote, they cast of the thyn paste thereon and so make a lytle cake in maner of a crakenell, or bysket.

The earliest reference cited here for 'krakenelle' is circa 1440. Weekley suggests that the surname Cracknell is a metonymic deriving from this confection, originally denoting someone who sold it, and he cites other examples of such as Pepper.

Just two examples of the surname Cracknell (or similar) have been found before 1600. As mentioned above, in 1220 Elias *de Crackenhal'* appeared in the Curia Regis Rolls of Yorkshire. (The Curia Regis was the King's council, established by William I (1066-1087); it was out of this council that the courts of the Common Pleas, Exchequer and King's Bench grew.) No further early examples have been found from Yorkshire.

Much later, Robert Craknell appears in the Suffolk Subsidy Rolls in 1524; the subsidy was a tax levied on possessions rather than land. Not all householders were included in this tax; if they were too poor to be taxed or only had possessions that were necessary to their work, they would be exempt.

Early examples of the surname Crackel, which is likely to share a common root in the place-names Crakehall and Crakehill, are rather more plentiful. Reaney and Wilson cite Alan *de Crachale* from Yorkshire Assize Rolls of 1204; and Thomas *Crakall* who was a Freeman of York in 1414. Our own survey has found a further example from *A Calendar to the Feet of Fines for London and Middlesex 1189-1485*. (The feet of fines was a means of conveying or settling freehold property, from the reign of Richard I up to 1834, when a Statute was passed to abolish the method and set up a simpler way of achieving matters.) The following reference to the name Crachale was found:

> Walter de Maddeley and Alice his wife and John de Crachale and Margaret his wife. A messuage in the parish of St Andrew's Hoeburn without the Bar. 55 Henry III (1270)

John de Crachale and his wife Margaret were thus acquiring a dwelling house in the parish of St Andrew's Holborn in London in 1270/1.

Given the sparseness of medieval evidence it is impossible to be certain that the surname Craknell, found in Suffolk in the 1520s, derived from a place-name in North Yorkshire. It is certainly possible that someone already bearing the surname migrated to Suffolk prior to this date; or that someone arrived in Suffolk from Crake(n)hall and was given the surname. However, the long gap between the clear example of a locative surname in Yorkshire in 1220, and the appearance of the surname in Suffolk three centuries later, means that we cannot entirely dismiss Ernest Weekley's suggestion as fanciful.

Distribution

The existing volumes of the English Surname Series (which is very incomplete) contain no references to the name in any form. This series includes the surnames of the West Riding of Yorkshire.

H R Moulton's *Palaeography, Genealogy and Topography* (primarily a sale catalogue printed in the 1930's listing historical documents, ancient charters, leases, court rolls, etc.) has been searched but no entries for the name Cracknell or variants were found.

In 1890 H B Guppy published his *Homes of Family Names in Great Britain*, still the only published work on surname distribution in Britain as a whole. His work was based on printed genealogies and a survey of county directories for the 1880s, in which he looked especially at the names of farmers, reasoning that they were among the most stable groups in society.

Guppy noted that there was a proportion of 39 in 10,000 farmers who bore the name Cracknell at that time in Suffolk. Guppy restricted his study to names which appeared in a proportion of 7:10,000 or higher. This signifies a cluster of the surname some distance from its suggested origins in Yorkshire, and it will be remembered that one of the two pre-1600 references to the name came from Suffolk.

C W Bardsley's *Dictionary of English and Welsh Surnames, with Special American Incidences* includes a survey of various directories, both English and American, from the nineteenth century. Bardsley lists one appearance of the name Cracknall in an 1870 London directory and thirteen Cracknells; there was also one Cracknell in an 1886 Boston directory.

George F Black in *The Surnames of Scotland* does not mention Cracknell or any variants. Nor did we find any reference to the name in T J Morgan and Prys Morgan's *Welsh Surnames*, or Edward MacLysaght's *Guide to Irish Surnames* or *The Surnames of Ireland*.

Many of the sources available for charting surname distribution through the centuries are necessarily confined to the wealthier sectors of the population: in general, nobody wanted to know the names of the poor but the names of those with money or land were naturally of interest to the authorities. However, one source that covers the whole of the social spectrum is provided by English parish registers, the earliest of which began in 1538 following a mandate that all parish priests should keep a weekly record of all baptisms, marriages and burials that took place in their parish. A survey of a cross section of parish registers for the years 1601 and 1602 was carried out in 1910 by F K and S Hitching; incidences of a particular surname are noted by parish and county, although with no indication of numbers of references. The name Cracknell or variants did not appear in either volume, again suggesting a strongly localised name which was rare nationally.

A useful guide to the distribution of surnames for the sixteenth, seventeenth and eighteenth centuries in England is provided by the indexes to wills proved, and administrations granted, at the Prerogative Court of (the

Archbishop of) Canterbury, in London, which had superior jurisdiction over local ecclesiastical courts where wills were proved until 1858. The PCC thus provides a national index, although it is not a completely representative one, as testators whose wills were proved in the PCC were mostly among the wealthier members of society, and a disproportionate number of them were from London or Middlesex.

A search of the indexes for the years 1584 to 1800 found the following entries for Cracknell, Cracknall and we have also included the surname Crackwell/Crakewell:

Seventeenth Century
1650   Thomas Cracknell, Great Stanmore, Middlesex
1696   John Cracknell, mariner HMS Royal William, Portsmouth, Hampshire

Eighteenth Century
1714   John Crackwell, Pts
1746   Thomas Langley Crakewell, Pts
1746   Benjamin Cracknell, Middx
1786   John Cracknell [of] "Eagle"
1793   Henry Cracknall, Essex

1800-1857
1804   Joseph Cracknell, victualler of Wimpole, Cambridgeshire
1806   Mary Cracknell, widow of Romford, Essex
1815   Thomas Cracknell, merchant seaman of Ealing, Middlesex
1822   Thomas Cracknell, gentleman of Colchester, Essex
1826   Richard Cracknell otherwise Crack, labourer of Bishops Stortford, Hertfordshire
1827   Thomas Cracknell, gardener of Enfield, Middlesex

1835   Stephen Cracknall, wheelwright of
           Woodditton, Cambridgeshire

1837   James Cracknall, breeches maker of Old Bond
           Street, Middlesex

1840   William Cracknell, market gardener of Enfield,
           Middlesex

1850   Simeon Cracknell, baker of Deptford, Kent

1857   George Cracknell, armourer sergeant no 1015 of
           Depot Battalion, Rifle Regiment of Foot

The PCC was the usual court used for testators who died abroad and there are two examples of this in this list. In 1714, John Crackwell and in 1746 Thomas Langley Crakewell, both died 'Pts' (*in partibus transmarinus*). Crackwell and Crakewell may be further variants of the surname Cracknell, or they may come from a difference source.

Cracknell was found in Middlesex and Hampshire in the seventeenth century and Middlesex and Essex in the eighteenth century. John Cracknell, whose will was proved in 1786, was a mariner of the ship 'Eagle'.

In the nineteenth century the most common variant was Cracknell with only two examples of Cracknall. The name was found predominately in Essex, Cambridgeshire and Middlesex. Surprisingly, in the light of Guppy's analysis, Suffolk is completely absent from this list.

For the nineteenth century, H B Guppy's survey has been mentioned above. Another important Victorian source is the *Return of Owners of Land of 1873*, sometimes known as the Modern Domesday Book. This source lists, county by county, every owner of an acre of land or more, with their residence (not necessarily the address of their property) and the acreage of their holding.

Return of Owners of Land

Cambridgeshire	1	Cracknell
Essex	1	Cracknell
Norfolk	1	Cracknell
Suffolk	13	Cracknell
Surrey	1	Cracknell

The name appears here only as Cracknell and it was found mainly in East Anglia with one appearance of the name in Surrey. The most occurrences of the name were found in Suffolk, where Guppy had found his farmers.

The first decennial census return in England, Scotland and Wales was taken in 1801, but personal information was only recorded from 1841 onwards. From 1851, the age, occupation and birthplace is given for each member of the household, and so these records provide invaluable genealogical information as well as a fascinating 'snapshot' of the family in the nineteenth century. The latest return currently open to public inspection is that of 1911 and there are now national indexes to the returns from 1841 onwards, although these indexes are not wholly reliable. Using these indexes, we found the following numbers for Cracknell, Cracknall and Crackwell in Channel Islands, England, Scotland (not 1911) and Wales:

6 **June 1841:**	Cracknell (1008), Cracknall (14), Crackwell (1)
30 **March 1851:**	Cracknell (1188), Cracknall (27), Crackwell (6)
7 **April 1861:**	Cracknell (1497), Cracknall (39), Crackwell (6)

11

2 April 1871:	Cracknell (1809), Cracknall (29), Crackwell (9)
3 April 1881:	Cracknell (2125), Cracknall (59), Crackwell (10)
5 April 1891:	Cracknell (2423), Cracknall (17), Crackwell (1)
31 March 1901:	Cracknell (2884), Cracknall (5), Crackwell (3)
2 April 1911:	Cracknell (3120), Cracknall (34), Crackwell (48)

Between 1841 and 1911 (a period in which the population was expanding rapidly) we see a steady growth in the numbers of entries for the surname Cracknell but Cracknall and Crackwell both fluctuate quite widely during this period. Some Cracknalls are likely to have been recorded as Cracknell (and possibly vice versa) and it is also likely that during the indexing process the forms Cracknell and Crackwell have been confused. It is clear, however, that the dominant form was Cracknell.

Famous bearers of the name

The *Dictionary of National Biography* for the British Isles has no references to anyone named Cracknell etc and there are no coats of arms listed in Burke's *General Armory* granted to men of the name Cracknell etc. We have also found no references to printed genealogies of Cracknell families but we noted with interest that a De Crakehall family genealogy appears in *Lincolnshire Notes & Queries* (ix, 55).

However, James Edward Cracknell OBE was a gold medallist in the Olympic Games in Sydney in 2000 and in Athens in 2004, rowing in the Coxless Four.

Summary

To conclude, the name Cracknell is a relatively uncommon surname of Old English origin, which appears to derive from a place-name *Cracanhale*. The only modern manifestations of this place-name are in the North Riding of Yorkshire, and here the very earliest reference to the surname has been found; however, by the sixteenth century the name was found in Suffolk, where it ramified. This suggests two possibilities: either a family or individual moved from Yorkshire to Suffolk (in which case all the modern Cracknells might possibly be related), or a similar place-name once existed in Suffolk, and has since been lost.

Sources Consulted

Mr Avenell, *The Norman People*, (London 1874)

C W Bardsley, *Dictionary of English and Welsh Surnames* (1901: reprinted, Baltimore: Genealogical Publishing Co, 1967)

Geoffrey B Barrow, *The Genealogist's Guide* (London: Research Publishing Co, 1977)

George F Black, *The Surnames of Scotland* (New York Public Library, 1946)

Charles Bridge, *An Index to Pedigrees* (London, 1867)

Burke's Family Index (London: Burke's Peerage Limited, 1976)

Sir Bernard Burke, *The General Armory* (London, 1884)

Indexes to 1841–1911 Census Returns of England and Wales (The National Archives/*Ancestry.com*)

The Concise Dictionary of National Biography, Part II, 1901–1950, (Oxford, 1961)

Debrett's People of Today (Debrett's Peerage Limited: London, 1996)

Debrett's Heraldry (London, 1933)

Eilert Ekwall, *The Concise Oxford Dictionary of English Place-names* (Oxford: Clarendon Press, 4th edition, 1960)

L'Estrange Ewen, *Guide to the Origin of British Surnames* (London: John Gifford, 1938)

CH B Guppy, Homes of Family Names in Great Britain (London, 1890)

W J Hardy & W Page, A Calendar to the Feet of Fines for London and Middlesex: Vol 1 Richard I – Richard III (1189–1485) (London, 1892)

P Hanks & F Hodges, *A Dictionary of Surnames* (Oxford University Press, 1988)

F K & S Hitching, *References to English Surnames in 1601* (Walton on Thames: Bernau, 1910)

F K & S Hitching, *References to English Surnames in 1602* (Walton on Thames: Bernau, 1911)

J P Brooke-Little, revised, *Boutell's Heraldry* (Frederick Warne: London, 1970)

M A Lower, *Patronymica Brittanica* (London, 1860)

Edward MacLysaght, *The Surnames of Ireland* (Dublin: Irish University Press, 1977)

G W Marshall, *The Genealogist's Guide* (1903; reprinted, Baltimore: GPC 1973)

Richard McKinley, *The Surnames of Oxfordshire* (English Surnames Series III: Leopard's Head Press, 1977)

Richard McKinley, *The Surnames of Sussex* (English Surnames Series V: Leopard's Head Press, 1988)

Richard McKinley, *The Surnames of Lancashire* (English Surnames Series IV: Leopard's Head Press, 1981)

Richard McKinley, *Norfolk and Suffolk Surnames in the Middle Ages* (English Surnames Series II: Phillimore, 1975)

T J & Prys Morgan, *Welsh Surnames* (Cardiff: University of Wales Press, 1985)

H R Moulton, *Palaeography, Genealogy & Topography* (Sale Catalogue, 1930)

The Oxford Dictionary of National Biography (online, 2004–2014)

Index to Prerogative Court of Canterbury Wills (The National Archives: online)

P H Reaney, *The Origins of English Surnames* (London: Routledge & Kegan Paul, 1967)

P H Reaney & R M Wilson, *A Dictionary of British Surnames* (Oxford: Oxford University Press, 3rd edition, 1995)

P H Reaney, *Dictionary of British Surnames* (London: Routledge & Kegan Paul, 2nd edition, 1976)

George Redmonds, *Yorkshire West Riding* (English Surnames Series I: Phillimore, 1973)

The Return of Owners of Land (1873)

ScotlandsPeople: Indexes to Old Parish Registers, Testaments, Statutory Registers

C R Humphrey-Smith, editor, *Burke's General Armory Volume II,* (Tabard Press, 1973)

Ernest Weekley, *The Romance of Names* (London: John Murray, 2nd edition, 1917)

Ernest Weekley, *Surnames* (London: John Murray, 1917)

E G Withycombe, *The Oxford Dictionary of English Christian Names* (Oxford: Clarendon Press, 2nd edition, 1950)

J B Whitmore, *A Genealogical Guide* (London, 1953)

Index to 1841-1911 census returns for England & Wales (Ancestry.co.uk)